BiBLe BRain BenDeRS

Lois Keffer
& Lindy Keffer

YOUR WORD IS A LAMP TO MY FEET AND A LIGHT FOR MY PATH.
PSALM 119:105

Bible Brain Benders for Road Trips
© 2006 Cook Communications Ministries

Authors: Lindy Keffer and Lois Keffer
Design and Illustration: Lois Keffer
Cover Design: Scott Johnson/BMB Design
Acquisitions Editor: Mary McNeil

Faith Kidz® is an imprint of Cook Communications Ministries
Colorado Springs, Colorado 80918
Cook Communications, Paris, Ontario
Kingsway Communications, Eastbourne, England

Summary: A puzzle book based on Bible stories.
ISBN: 0-7814-4350-4
First printing, 2006

1 2 3 4 5 6 7 8 9 10 Printing/Year 10 09 08 07 06
Printed in USA

ready or not ...

it's road trip season!

Just think of the fun in store for you ...

... seeing how many times you can ask, "Are we there yet?" before you get yelled at.

... making every meal stop miserable because you want to eat some-place different from everyone else.

... annoying your sibling, asking for potty stops every five min-utes, begging for ice cream in every town ...

the possibilities are endless!

or

You could have some major fun, make the miles fly by, amaze your family, get to know the Bible a lot better, AND keep those brain cells firing so you're not completely clueless when school (gasp!) starts again in the fall.

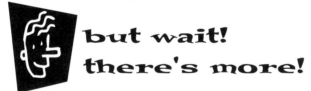

but wait! there's more!

It's not only painless, it's FUN! You'll get to tackle all kinds of great puzzles and challenges that will bend your brain, needle your neurons, freak out your funny bone, and build up your Bible smarts.

So buckle up, because you're about to join some of the greatest Bible road trips on record. Grab a pencil and prepare to be amazed at the fun and adventure ahead.

(By the way, it's fair to ask others in the car for help. After all, you don't want to be the only brilliant one in the family!)

Lindy and Lois

ABRAHAM
DESTINATION UNKNOWN

When your family sets out on a road trip, you usually know exactly where you're going. If it's some place familiar, like Grandma's house, you know all the best roadside stops and exactly how long it takes to get there. Maybe you're off to your favorite camping spot or a theme park. When you get all your gear in the car, you've got one thing in mind: getting there!

Suppose a moving van pulled up at your neighbor's house one day. You drop by to ask where the neighbors are moving and they answer, "We have no clue. We're just gonna head out and see where the road takes us."

Guess what. That's exactly what Abraham did. (We'll talk later about his name change.) Check out Genesis 12. God came to Abraham and said, "Get packing!" He told Abraham to leave his home and set out for ... somewhere. God promised to show the way, but it was up to Abe to get the caravan together, pack the camels, and explain to his curious neighbors that he was leaving his comfy life behind without a clue about his final destina-tion.

So began a great journey of faith across deserts and through exotic lands. Abraham would be welcomed by kings, gain wealth, fight desperate battles, participate in a risky charade, and split with a close relative. The destination and even what happened along the way wasn't nearly as important to Abraham as God's promise to be with him. That's why he's one of the Bible's greatest heroes.

The Bible tells us that when we show the kind of trust Abraham did, we become sons and daughters of Abraham through faith. So let's hit the road with Abe and Sarah, taking this promise from Genesis 12:2–3 with us.

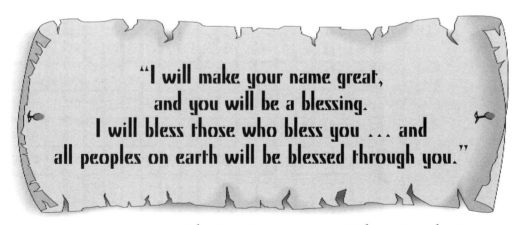

"I will make your name great,
and you will be a blessing.
I will bless those who bless you ... and
all peoples on earth will be blessed through you."

That's quite a passport! Why not make it your own?
Travel in faith, and ask God to bless others through you.

Abraham's Journey

Following God's guidance, Abraham visited and lived in places all over the Middle East. He met famous people and had all kinds of adventures. Find the words from Abraham's story in Genesis 12–15 hidden in the puzzle below. The words may run forward or backward and horizontally, vertically, or diagonally.

Word List

blessing
Abram
Sarai
Lot
Haran
Canaan
Egypt
pharaoh
camel
Negev
flocks
herds
Sodom
altar
promise
Lord
kings
land

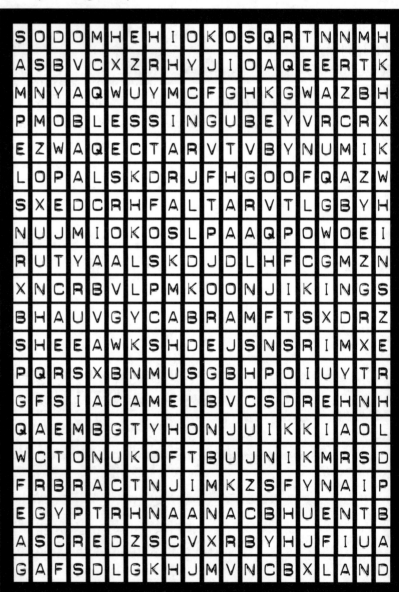

You'll find the answers on p. 70.

Too Many to Count

Even though Abraham didn't have children yet, God told him that he would eventually have a family so big that no one could count it. It took a while, but God gave Abraham a son named Isaac. Through Isaac, Abraham's family grew and grew. How long do you think it took before the number was uncountable? No one can say for sure, but this math puzzler will show you how fast descendants can multiply.

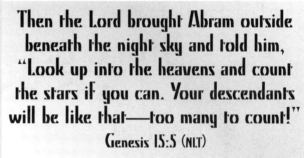

Then the Lord brought Abram outside beneath the night sky and told him, "Look up into the heavens and count the stars if you can. Your descendants will be like that—too many to count!"
Genesis 15:5 (NLT)

If a man named John has two children by the time he is twenty-five years old, and each of them has two children by age twenty-five, and each of those children has two children by age twenty-five, and so on, how long will it take for John's family to grow to one million descendants?

hint:

Complete this table to figure out how many generations it will take, then multiply that number by twenty-five to get the number of years.

Generation	Number of descendants in this generation	Total number of people in the family
0 John	0	1
1 John's kids	2	3
2 John's grandkids	4	7
3 John's great-grandkids	8	15

You'll find the answer on p. 70.

Egyptian Mind Bender

When they arrived in Egypt, perhaps Abraham put four of his servants, whom we'll call

Shua, Beruch, Gad, and Hosea,

in charge of his four different types of livestock:

 cattle, sheep, camels, and goats.

Using the clues below, see if you can figure out which servant cared for which kind of animal.

1. Hosea was responsible for shearing his animals' wool.

2. Gad was glad that he didn't have to care for the camels, because he didn't like the way they spit.

3. Shua's favorite part of his job was caring for the calves when they were born.

4. Beruch got spit on by one of the animals in his care.

Big Hint:

Use the grid below to keep track of what you know.

For example, from fact #1, you can figure out that Hosea kept the sheep. So put a "yes" in the "sheep" box under Hosea's name. Then put "no" in the sheep box under everyone else's name, since only one person kept sheep.

Also, put "no" in every other animal's space under Hosea's name, since you know he cared for only one type of animal.

Keep filling in boxes like this until you bend your brain cells around the whole solution.

	Shua	Beruch	Gad	Hosea
cattle				
sheep				
camel				
goats				

 You'll find the answers on p. 70.

YOUR ROYAL WHO-NESS?

One of the adventures on Abraham's road trip was a battle that involved nine kings. And those kings had really weird names. See how many words you can make from the letters in each of their names.

Amraphel of Shinar

Examples: ram, arm, lap, shine

_____

Arioch of Ellasar

_____

Kedorlaomer of Elam

_____

Tidal of Goiim

_____

Bera of Sodom

_____

Birsha of Gomorrah

_____

Shinab of Admah

_____

Shemeber of Zeboiim

_____

Mix it up! Make this puzzle a contest. Challenge a friend or family member to see who can come up with the most words from each king's name and city.

SWITCHEROOS

Abram fell facedown, and God said to him, "As for me, this is my covenant with you: You will be the father of many nations. No longer will you be called Abram; your name will be Abraham, for I have made you a father of many nations."

During their road trip, our travelers were called Abram and Sarai. But life-changing events called for new names, and God had just the right names in mind. Check out these name switcheroos from Genesis 17: 3–5, 15–16.

Abe and Sarah aren't the only Bible people who got new names. After each clue, fill in each name changer's old and new names.

1. This traveler got knocked over by a bright light on the road to Damascus. (Acts 9:1–9; 13:9)

Old name: _____

New name: _____

2. Pharaoh invaded from Egypt. He made this guy king of Judah and gave him a new name. (2 Kings 23:34)

Old name: _____

New name: _____

"As for Sarai your wife, you are no longer to call her Sarai; her name will be Sarah. I will bless her and will surely give you a son by her. I will bless her so that she will be the mother of nations; kings of peoples will come from her."

3. This man wrestled with God beside a stream. (Genesis 32:22–28)

Old name: _____

New name: _____

4. Nebuchadnezzar, king of Babylon, switched kings in Judah and gave this king a new name. (2 Kings 24:15–17)

Old name: _____

New name: _____

5. This disciple said he believed Jesus was the Son of God. (Matthew 16:15–19)

Old name: _____

New name: _____

6. This person gets a new name in heaven. SURPRISE! (Revelation 2:17)

Old name: _____

New name: _____

You'll find the answers on p. 70.

NORTH AND SOUTH

The Lord said to Abram ... "Lift up your eyes from where you are and look north and south, east and west. All the land that you see I will give to you and your offspring forever. I will make your offspring like the dust of the earth, so that if anyone could count the dust, then your offspring could be counted. Go, walk through the length and breadth of the land, for I am giving it to you."

Genesis 13:14–17

Walk with Abraham through the land God promised him.

Wherever the directions say to walk, use your pencil to draw a line. When you are done, you will see how one of Abraham's descendants showed his love for the world.

DIRECTIONS

1. Walk 2 spaces to the east.
2. Walk 4 spaces to the south.
3. Walk 5 spaces to the east.
4. Walk 2 spaces to the south.
5. Walk 5 spaces to the west.
6. Walk 11 spaces to the south.
7. Walk 2 spaces to the west.
8. Walk 11 spaces to the north.
9. Walk 5 spaces to the west.
10. Walk 2 spaces to the north.
11. Walk 5 spaces to the east.
12. Walk 4 spaces to the north.

You'll find the solution on p. 71.

START →

THE EXODUS
ROAD TRIP THROUGH THE DESERT

It all started with Joseph. When his brothers sold him to be a slave in Egypt, they didn't know they were starting something big. Joseph had his ups and downs, but God saw to it that everything ended on a big up, with Joseph second in command of all Egypt.

Joseph brought his whole family to live in Egypt. They had children, and their children had children, until there were more than a million of them. Seeing how God blessed the Israelites, the Egyptians grew fearful. They thought the day might come when the Israelites would try to take over.

That's when the Egyptians got the bright idea of making the Israelites serve them as slaves.

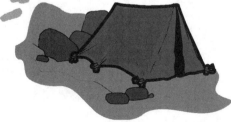

Suppose someone made you a slave. What do you think life would be like? What kinds of jobs would you have to do?

For the Israelites, slavery meant building huge cities for Pharaoh. The slavemasters were cruel. God's people cried to him for help, and he heard them. He sent Moses to tell Pharaoh, "Let my people go."

Pharaoh needed a lot of convincing, but God was more than up to the job. God sent ten plagues on the Egyptians. In the middle of a terrible night when all the firstborn sons of Egypt died, Pharaoh finally agreed to let the Israelites go.

The Israelites' road trip was a LONG one. It took more than two years to reach the border of the Promised Land. They faced hunger, thirst, and vicious enemies. With each challenge they learned to trust in God to take care of their needs and protect them. When they reached the Promised Land, the Israelites sent spies to scope it out. Ten of the twelve spies reported that the people who lived there were too powerful to be defeated. The Israelites freaked out and refused to move ahead. Oops!

> "I will walk among you and be your God, and you will be my people. I am the LORD your God, who brought you out of Egypt so that you would no longer be slaves to the Egyptians."
>
> Leviticus 26:12–13

So, the long road trip turned into an even longer one. The consequence for disobeying God was wandering in the desert for forty years—until all the grown-ups had died. Only then could the Israelites go home to the land God had promised Abraham so long ago.

We're So Outta

When Pharaoh said, "Take your people and go," he didn't have to repeat himself! The Israelites had followed God's directions, and they were ready to hit the road. See if you know the story well enough to solve this crossword.

Down

1. Ruler of Egypt, keeper of slaves
2. Talked to God in a burning bush
3. Moses' big bro
4. Offer an animal to God
6. Who died in the final plague?
7. Only plague that involved ice
9. What the Israelites were to the Egyptians
10. Sent Aaron and Moses to free the Israelites
13. Plague that kept the Egyptians from seeing things right in front of them
17. Animal to be sacrificed on Passover

Across

2. Tried to do the same miracles as Moses and Aaron
5. The ten different punishments God sent on the Egyptians
6. The plague with lots of hopping and croaking
8. Body of water the Israelites walked through (2 words)
11. What Aaron used to perform miracles
12. Plague that made the river stink
14. Who carried out the plague on the firstborn?
15. Moses wanted Pharoah to set the Israelites _____.
16. River mentioned in the Exodus story

Here Crossword

You'll find the answers on p. 71.

CARRY ON

The Israelites traveled for years and years on their way to the Promised Land. Everywhere they went, they had to carry all the things they'd brought with them from Egypt.

In the family of **simeon**,

mary carried money and meat;

hadassah carried honey, head-coverings, and hides;

reuben carried robes, rings, and rolls.

In the family of **joshua**,

aaron carried olives, almonds, and opals;

samuel carried a walking stick, rope, and a basket;

elizabeth carried earrings, oils, and eggs;

tamar carried spices, blankets, and tent pegs.

Some families had special rules about who could carry what. From the clues in the boxes, can you figure out each family's rule?

You'll find the answers on p. 71.

WHINE-ATHON

People on long trips sometimes get grumpy. (We wouldn't be talking about anyone in your car, of course.)

The Israelites loved their whine time. They complained about the food. They complained about not having enough water. They complained about Moses, their leader. In fact, even though God faithfully took care of them, their whole trip to the Promised Land turned out to be a whine-athon!

The words below aren't from an ancient biblical language. They're scrambled phrases that might sound familiar if you've ever had the whinies on a road trip. See if you can unscramble them.

1. rea ew reeht ety?

_____

2. nac ew pots orf hcnul?

_____

3. i veha ot og ot het mrohtabo!

_____

4. mi' edrbo!

_____

5. sh'e niuhcotg em!

_____

You'll find the answers on p. 71.

EXODUS BY THE NUMBERS

Go on a number hunt through the book of Exodus to find the answers to the following questions. When you've filled in all the answers, do the math! If you're a whiz-bang mathemaniac, you'll end up with the answer that's printed. If you're off, crunch the numbers again.

And remember, you can always count on God's Word!

A. Aaron's age when he spoke to Pharaoh (Exodus 7:7) _____

B. The number of days Moses wanted the people to hold a festival to God in the wilderness (Exodus 5:3) _____

C. The number of years Levi lived (Exodus 6:16) _____

D. The number of plagues God sent (Exodus 7:19—11:10) _____

E. The number of male Israelites who left Egypt (Exodus 12:37) _____

F. The number of years the Israelites were in slavery in Egypt (Exodus 12:40) _____

G. The numer of chariots Pharaoh used to chase the Israelites after they left Egypt (Exodus 14:7) _____

H. The number of commandments God gave Moses on Mount Sinai (Exodus 20:2–17) _____

A - B = _____

+ C = _____

x D = _____

+ E = _____

- F = _____

- G = _____

÷ H = _____ **60,114**

You'll find the answers on p. 71.

STONES OF REMEMBRANCE

When the Israelites were ready at last to enter the Promised Land, God split another body of water—the rushing Jordan River—so the entire nation could walk through. After they finished crossing, God told them to carry large rocks from the river bed to the Promised Land as a set-in-stone reminder of God's river-stopping power.

Make words from the letters on the stones. Write them in a sentence that tells the message of the stones from the Jordan River. You'll use one word twice.

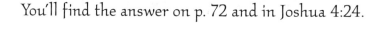

You'll find the answer on p. 72 and in Joshua 4:24.

THE LONG WAY HOME

Shortcuts are great. But because the Israelites responded with fear and disobedience when they first came to the Promised Land, God gave them a "longcut." He sent them wandering in the desert for forty years. Talk about taking the long way home! See if you can guide the Israelites safely through the maze and back to the Promised Land.

The Big Ten

When Moses climbed Mount Sinai to meet with God, God gave him the Ten Commandments. God gave these commandments because he cared for his people and wanted them to live wisely. Here are the first four commandments from Exodus 20:2–8 (NLT). They tell how God expected the people to treat him.

1. I AM THE LORD YOUR GOD, WHO RESCUED YOU FROM SLAVERY IN EGYPT. DO NOT WORSHIP ANY OTHER GODS BESIDES ME.

2. DO NOT MAKE IDOLS OF ANY KIND.

3. DO NOT MISUSE THE NAME OF THE LORD YOUR GOD.

4. REMEMBER TO OBSERVE THE SABBATH DAY BY KEEPING IT HOLY.

Hundreds of years later, people asked Jesus which was the most important commandment. Crack the code to discover how Jesus answered.

___ ___ ___ ___ the ___ ___ ___ ___ with ___ ___ ___
1-7, 2-2, 4-16, 3-11   1-7, 1-8, 1-9, 1-10   1-2, 1-36, 1-36

___ ___ ___ ___ ___ ___ ___ ___ ___ and ___ ___ ___ ___
2-19, 3-2, 1-13, 4-1   4-19, 3-11, 1-2, 4-8, 1-4   1-18, 2-10, 1-4, 4-19

all ___ ___ ___ ___ ___ ___ ___ ___ ___ ___ ___ with
     2-19, 3-2, 1-13, 4-1   2-14, 2-2, 3-9, 1-7   1-2, 3-3, 3-1

___ ___ ___ ___ ___ ___ ___ ___ ___ ___ ___.
4-22, 2-13, 2-13   3-28, 3-29, 3-30, 3-31   1-3, 3-7, 3-15, 1-17

Hint: Notice how the first number in each pair matches the number of one of the first four commandments.

Was that one too easy for you?

Here are the final six commandments from Exodus 20:12–17 (NLT). They teach how God expected his people to treat each other.

5. HONOR YOUR FATHER AND MOTHER. THEN YOU WILL LIVE A LONG, FULL LIFE IN THE LAND THE LORD YOUR GOD WILL GIVE YOU.

6. DO NOT MURDER.

7. DO NOT COMMIT ADULTERY.

8. DO NOT STEAL.

9. DO NOT TESTIFY FALSELY AGAINST YOUR NEIGHBOR.

10. DO NOT COVET.

Jesus summed up these six commandments in just five words. But to discover what he said, you'll have to crack another code. Go for it!

$\overline{}$ $\overline{}$ $\overline{}$
FIPY SIOL HYCABVIL

$\overline{}$ $\overline{}$
UM SIOLMYFZ

Hint: Which commandment keeps people from killing one another? The number of that commandment will help you create a decoder to solve this puzzle.

You'll find the answers on p. 72.

TO EXILE AND BACK

The truth is, the Israelites just didn't get it. You'd think after the way God brought them out of Egypt, then took care of all their needs in the wilderness for forty years, they might have gotten a clue about trusting God and obeying him. When God finally allowed them to enter the land, he was there to help them defeat their enemies, just as he'd promised.

Then the Israelites built a kingdom. Before long, they wanted a king like all the other nations had. So God gave them kings. Some kings were good and honored God's laws. But there were evil kings who worshipped the false god Baal. When Baal worship spread across the country, God sent prophets to warn the people that their unfaithfulness would be punished. But the Israelites paid no attention.

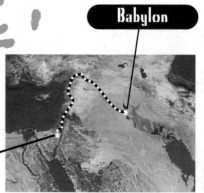

Babylon

Jerusalem

Then the mighty armies of Assyria and Babylonian defeated God's people. They burned the city of Jerusalem, broke down its walls, and took the people to exile. Another road trip. And this one was no leisurely vacation. The Hebrew captives were marched eight hundred miles to be slaves and servants. They were given foreign names and had to learn a strange language. No one would be allowed to return to the land of Israel for seventy years.

But even in a faraway land, God was faithful to the Israelites. He told them to settle down and build new lives in Babylon. He promised that while they were in exile he would remember them with his constant love. As he always does, God kept that promise. He gave his people wisdom and protection and made them prosper. God used captives like Daniel, Shadrach, Meshach, and Abednego to make himself known among people who had never heard of him. After many years passed, God finally brought his people back to the Promised Land.

What about you? Do you believe that God will take care of you wherever you go? Are you willing to introduce him to people you meet along your journey?

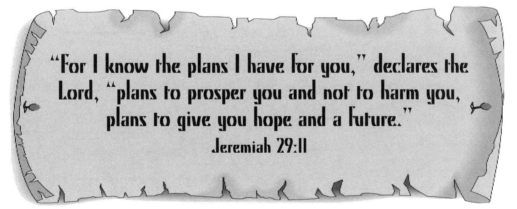

"For I know the plans I have for you," declares the Lord, "plans to prosper you and not to harm you, plans to give you hope and a future."

Jeremiah 29:11

Let's go with the Israelites on their road trip to exile and back and see what God has in store for you!

carried away

How well do you know the people you're traveling with? Pretty well, you say? Let's see!

When the Babylonians took the Hebrew people captive, there probably wasn't much time to prepare for a long journey to an unknown land. Ask your friends and family these questions to hear their interesting answers. If you're on a long road trip yourself, it's a good way to pass the time and get to know the people around you better.

You are suddenly taken captive and carried away on a long journey. You can carry only what will fit in a backpack.

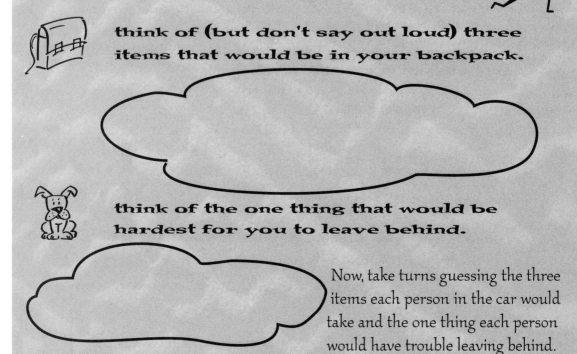

think of (but don't say out loud) three items that would be in your backpack.

think of the one thing that would be hardest for you to leave behind.

Now, take turns guessing the three items each person in the car would take and the one thing each person would have trouble leaving behind.

How well do you know each other?

settle down!

Once the Hebrew people got to their destination, it was a while before they could come back again to the Promised Land. So God told them to settle in for a while, build houses, and get comfortable.

> This is what the Lord Almighty, the God of Israel, says to
> all those I carried into exile from Jerusalem to Babylon:
> "Build houses and settle down;
> plant gardens and eat what they produce."
> Jeremiah 29:4–5

These four guys did just that. See if you can draw line to help each one get to the point of the roof of his house without crossing anyone else's path. Only one line may go between each house.

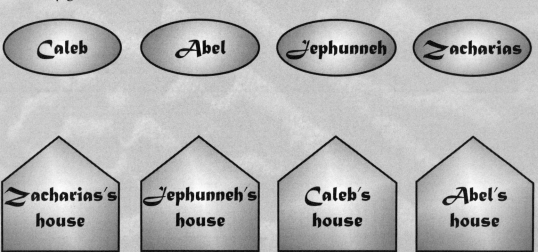

Caleb   Abel   Jephunneh   Zacharias

Zacharias's house   Jephunneh's house   Caleb's house   Abel's house

You'll find the solution on p. 72.

ALL THE KING'S MEN

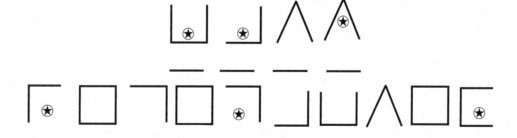

When King Nebuchadnezzar invaded Jerusalem, he took some of the most promising young men to his palace to be trained. Among them were Daniel, Shadrach, Meshach, and Abednego. The king ordered them to have the best food and drink. The problem was, the king's food had been sacrificed to false gods. Daniel and his friends didn't want to dishonor the true God by eating it.

So the young Israelites asked for a special diet. At first, their trainer said no—he was afraid Daniel and his friends would look scrawny and the king would get mad. But Daniel talked him into it. Sure enough, at the end of ten days, Daniel and his friends looked better than all the young men who ate the king's food, because God had blessed them. Use the decoder below to discover what Daniel and his friends ate.

DECODER

A	B	C		J		N⭐	O⭐	P⭐		W⭐
D	E	F	K	M		Q⭐	R⭐	S⭐	X⭐	Z⭐
G	H	I	L			T⭐	U⭐	V⭐		Y⭐

You'll find the answer on p. 73.

Raaaaaaarrr!

Getting buff on veggies wasn't the only amazing thing Daniel did. By God's power, he also survived a plot by jealous leaders that made him lion bait for a whole night. But Daniel prayed, and God closed the lions' mouths. Then his enemies ended up in the lions' den, and suddenly the big cats got their appetites back.

Would your faith get unscrambled in the face of hungry lions? Daniel's didn't! Try your paw at unscrambling these words and phrases about lions.

1. NEMA _____

2. PRASH LAWCS _____

3. TOPHIY ETTEH _____

4. TAC MLAFIY _____

5. GIKN FO SEBATS _____

6. FIRAAC _____

7. BCUS _____

You'll find the answers on p. 73.

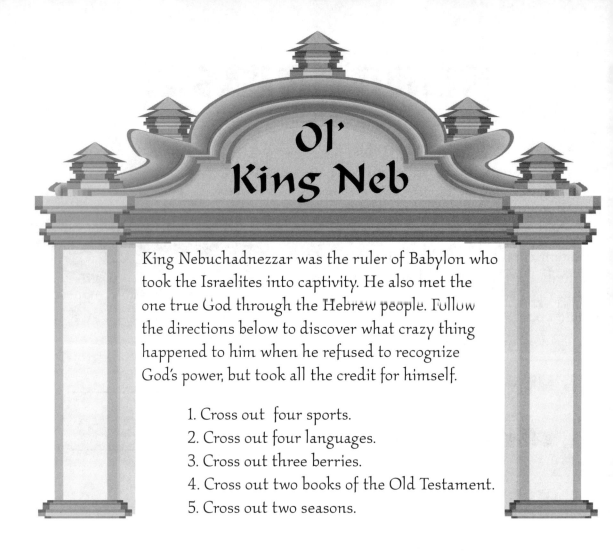

Ol' King Neb

King Nebuchadnezzar was the ruler of Babylon who took the Israelites into captivity. He also met the one true God through the Hebrew people. Follow the directions below to discover what crazy thing happened to him when he refused to recognize God's power, but took all the credit for himself.

1. Cross out four sports.
2. Cross out four languages.
3. Cross out three berries.
4. Cross out two books of the Old Testament.
5. Cross out two seasons.

He Basketball English Genesis Spanish Baseball Lived Blueberry Winter Strawberry German Like Tennis Russian An Raspberry Leviticus Animal Summer Soccer.

Check your answer on p. 73. Then read the whole story in Daniel 4.

There and Back Again

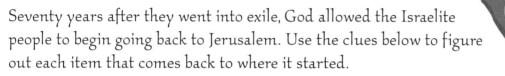

Seventy years after they went into exile, God allowed the Israelite people to begin going back to Jerusalem. Use the clues below to figure out each item that comes back to where it started.

Australia, throw, wood

_____

return to sender, postal service

_____

canine, fetch, golden

_____

diamond, hit, run, homer

_____

winter, fly south, honk

_____

You'll find the answers on p. 73.

CRACKED UP!

When the people of Israel got back to Jerusalem, their most important job was rebuilding the temple and the city walls, which had been destroyed when the people were taken captive. As they were working, some of the stones broke and couldn't be used.

The object of this game is not to get left with the broken stone. Let your partner cross out as many stones as he or she wants in one row. Then you do the same—crossing out the stones you pick, either in the same row as your partner or a different one, until only the broken stone is left. The person who must cross out the broken stone loses.

Play three matches and see if your strategy improves!

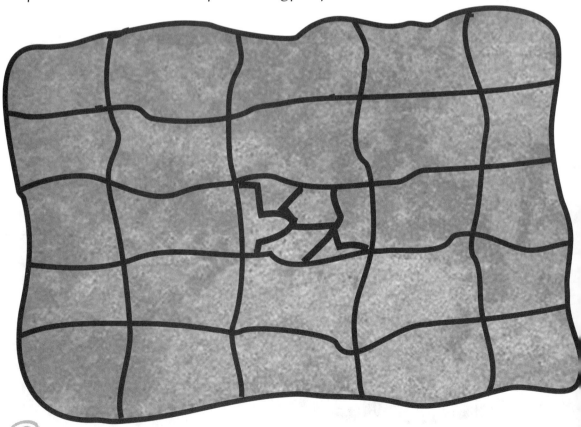

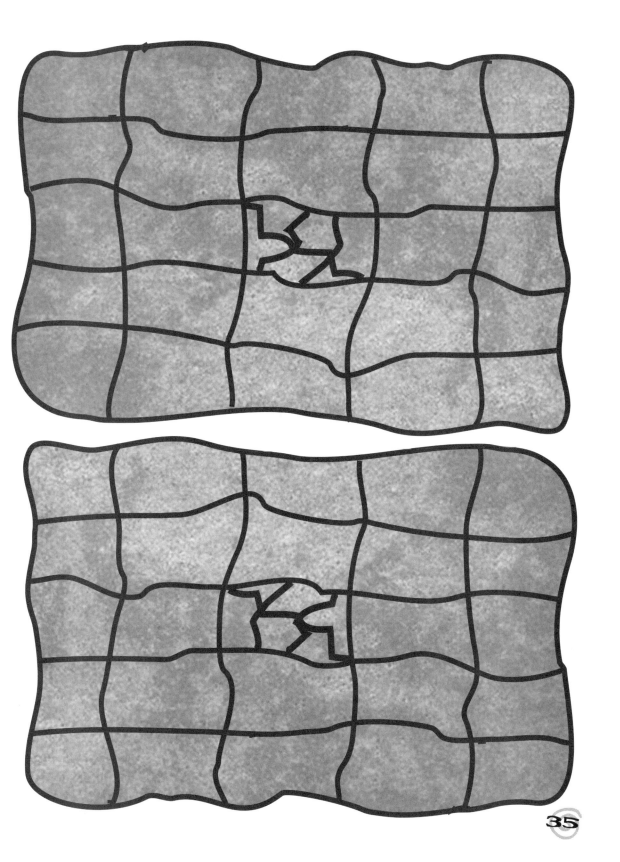

35

WALKING WHERE JESUS WALKED

You've probably heard the Christmas story so many times that you could tell it in your sleep. But think about it. God himself left heaven and came to earth as a baby. Talk about the ultimate road trip!

And that's not the last journey Jesus took, not by a long shot. When Jesus was a baby, an angel warned Joseph to take Mary and baby Jesus to Egypt to escape the murderous plans of evil King Herod. At age twelve, Jesus made the trip to Jerusalem to celebrate the Passover feast. Though his parents thought he had been left behind, he was at the temple amazing the priests and teachers of the Law with his knowledge of God's Word.

The Bible doesn't give us many windows into Jesus' life as a young man, except to say that he "grew in wisdom and stature, and in favor with God and men" (Luke 2:52).

Jesus began his public ministry at age thirty. He chose twelve men to be his disciples. Together they traveled around Lake Galilee. Jesus healed the sick, fed the hungry, taught about the kingdom of God, and introduced people to his Father's love.

It didn't take long for word about Jesus' power, his miracles, and his message of God's love to draw crowds wherever he went. The religious leaders in Jerusalem saw Jesus as a threat to their power and authority. Jesus knew what was coming when he traveled to Jerusalem. The crowds that welcomed him as king on Sunday would call for his death before the week was out.

> "I am the gate; whoever enters through me will be saved. He will come in and go out, and find pasture.... I have come that they may have life, and have it to the full."
> John 10:9–10

It was Jesus' love for you that led him on his final journey—the one to the cross. Knowing that he went there for you, will you follow him wherever he leads you?

THE SURPRISING SAVIOR

Jesus' trip to earth was full of surprises. Everything that people thought he would be, he wasn't. They thought he would show up as a strong ruler, but he showed up as a baby. They thought he would live in a palace, but he was born in a manger.

For each word listed below, give its opposite. Then, take the first letter of each opposite and fill it in below to discover a surprising thing Jesus said while he was on earth.

1. MOON ___ ___ ___

2. DIFFICULT ___ ___ ___ ___

3. COMMON ___ ___ ___ ___

4. PEACEFUL ___ ___ ___ ___ ___ ___ ___

5. NONE ___ ___ ___

6. ALWAYS ___ ___ ___ ___ ___

7. WONDERFUL ___ ___ ___ ___ ___ ___ ___ ___

Many people think that if you're a great person, you can make other people do what you want them to do. But Jesus said if you want to be great, you need to become a ___ ___ ___ ___ ___ ___ .

You'll find the answers on p. 73.

When Jesus was a baby, his earthly father, Joseph, was warned by God through a dream that Jesus was in danger, so he took Jesus and Mary and made tracks to Egypt. There, Jesus would be protected.

Rearrange the letters in these footprints to discover how Joseph knew it was safe to come back from Egypt.

__ __ __ __ __ __ __ __

__ __ __ __ __

E A E R E M D H N O A R T

You'll find the answer on p. 73.

Good Question!

Like all good Jewish rabbis, Jesus often answered people's questions with more questions. Here's an example from the book of Matthew. The other rabbis were trying to trap Jesus into saying something that would make people angry. Check out the way Jesus handled it.

The Question

Jesus entered the temple courts, and, while he was teaching, the chief priests and the elders of the people came to him. "By what authority are you doing these things?" they asked. "And who gave you this authority?"

Matthew 21:23

Jesus Answered with a Question

Jesus replied, "I will also ask you one question. If you answer me, I will tell you by what authority I am doing these things. John's baptism—where did it come from? Was it from heaven, or from men?"

Matthew 21:24–25

Good Question!

Can you think like a rabbi, the way Jesus did? On the line below each question, write another question that helps the reader know the answer to the first question. An example is done for you.

Q1. What state's capital is named Juneau?

Q2. What is the largest state in the United States?

The second question helps uncover the answer to the first, since they're the same thing. (By the way, the answer is Alaska!)

Now, you try it!

Q1. Do you like to dance?

Q2. _____

Q1. Which do you like better, dogs or cats?

Q2. _____

Q1. What is the weather like today?

Q2. _____

Q1. During what month is your birthday?

Q2. _____

When Jesus traveled and taught and healed people, huge crowds followed him. After a while, they would get hungry, but they didn't want to leave and miss what Jesus had to say. Jesus cared about the hungry people, so a couple of times he did a miracle and fed them all.

You'll need your Bible and your math smarts to work out the numbers on these amazing miracles. Get started by checking out Matthew 14:13–21.

A. Number of men in the first large crowd Jesus fed _____

B. Number of loaves of bread Jesus used to feed them _____

C. Number of fish in that meal _____

D. Number of baskets of leftovers the disciples picked up _____

Now take a look at Matthew 15:29–39.

E. Number of men in the second large crowd Jesus fed _____

F. Number of loaves of bread Jesus used to feed them _____

G. Number of baskets of leftovers the disciples picked up _____

FOOD?

During these crowd-feeding miracles, Jesus fed nine thousand men, but there were also women and children. If there was one woman or child for each man he fed, how many total people would Jesus have fed? Math whiz your way to the amazing answer!

$$A = \underline{\hspace{3cm}}$$
$$\div\ B = \underline{\hspace{3cm}}$$
$$\div\ C = \underline{\hspace{3cm}}$$
$$x\ 9 = \underline{\hspace{3cm}}$$
$$+\ D = \underline{\hspace{3cm}}$$
$$-\ E = \underline{\hspace{3cm}}$$
$$+\ 13 = \underline{\hspace{3cm}}$$
$$\div\ F = \underline{\hspace{3cm}}$$
$$-\ D = \underline{\hspace{3cm}}$$
$$-\ G = \underline{\hspace{3cm}}$$
$$-\ D = \underline{\hspace{3cm}}$$
$$+\ 1 = \underline{\hspace{3cm}}$$
$$x\ 400 = \underline{\hspace{3cm}}$$

(the number of people Jesus might have fed)

You'll find the answer on p. 74.

TWELVE FOR THE ROAD

When Jesus began his ministry, he picked twelve guys to travel with him as he walked around the countryside and taught about God's love. It's great to have buddies to travel with! See if you can answer these questions about your companions.

1. Which person has visited the greatest number of states?

2. Which person falls alseep fastest?

3. If each person could pick a car or truck, what would it be?

4. Who can be the first person to spot a green truck?

5. What does each person like to listen to in the car?

6. Who can read in the car without getting sick?

7. Who snores?

8. What is each person's favorite car snack?

seventy-two

Near the end of his journey on earth, Jesus chose more friends—in addition to his twelve disciples—and sent them on a road trip to other towns to heal people and tell them about his kingdom. He chose seventy-two friends to do this.

This is a game of seventy-two. Below are seventy-two squares—one for each of the friends Jesus sent on a journey. Invite one of your friends to play with you. You should take turns putting your initials in one, two, or three of the squares. The squares you choose on each turn should be in a row horizontally, vertically, or diagonally. Whoever puts his or her initials in the last square is the winner.

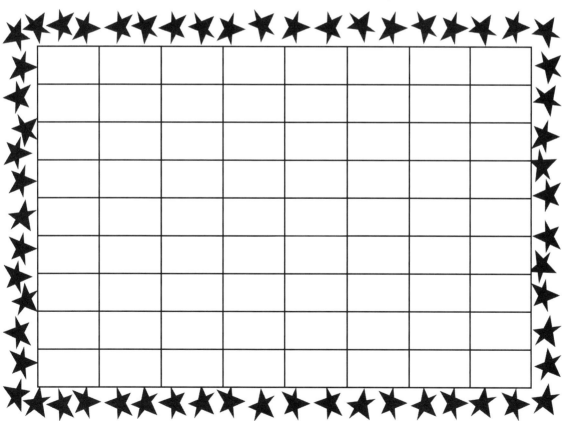

The Hardest Road

As Jesus' journey on earth neared its end, he knew he would have to walk toward Jerusalem, where he would be crucified for the sins of the world. It was the most difficult trip he ever had to make, but he did it willingly, because he loves you and me. Because he chose to make that difficult journey, everyone who accepts his gift of eternal life can one day take an amazing road trip to heaven!

Along the road to Calvary and the cross, Jesus met many people. Unscramble their names below.

1. Sicadj Utsaoir

_____

2. Teepr

_____

3. Lippton Suitea

_____

4. Ram Gdyalmanee

_____

5. Rbbbaaas

_____

6. Mcyern eisfr Onom

_____

You'll find the answers on p. 74.

Across

1. Jesus carried his own _____.
3. A Jewish teacher (Jesus was one.)
4. Preparing the way for Jesus, John told folks to _____ and be baptized.
5. Where Joseph and Mary hid to save baby Jesus from Herod.
8. Jesus was both God and ____.
10. Like the animals in the Old Testament, Jesus was _____ for sin.
11. What held Jesus to the cross
12. "The Son of Man did not come to be served, but to _____."

Down

1. Holiday when we celebrate Jesus' birth
2. Where Jesus walked on water (3 words)
4. He is _____ indeed!
6. Jesus came to _____ people about God's love
7. Jesus ____ and rose again
9. A supernatural happening
12. One who brings salvation
13. Jesus' heavenly Father

PAUL'S GREAT ADVENTURES

Have you ever traveled with a grump? It's no fun! They complain, have a bad attitude, and make life difficult for everyone. And Saul, whose journey we're about to explore, was a major grump.

It hadn't been long since Jesus had died and been raised to life again. Those who believed he was the Son of God and the Savior of the world were growing in number. But Saul didn't like them. And he would stop at nothing—even murder!—to make trouble for people who believed in Jesus.

But God turned the tables on Saul. While he was on his way to Damascus to arrest the Christians there, he had an enlightening experience. Literally.

A brilliant light shone down from heaven and knocked him flat on the ground and left him blind. And that's how Saul met Jesus.

The Christians in Damascus knew Saul was trouble, but God had spoken to Ananias and told him to welcome Saul. Ananias healed Saul's eyes and taught him what it means to have faith in Jesus.

Along with new life in Jesus, Saul got a new name—Paul—and a new travel agenda. He would spend the rest of his life traveling the world and preaching about Jesus. And boy, did he have his share of adventures—shipwrecks, nasty crowds, poisonous snakes, prisons, and earthquakes. You name it, and it happened to Paul. But Paul thought it was a privilege to spread the Good News, no matter what he had to face to do it.

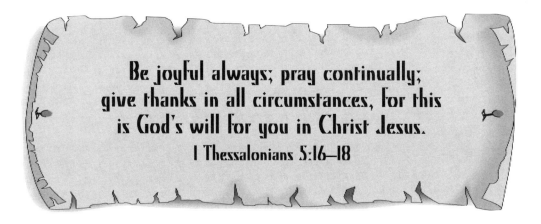

Be joyful always; pray continually; give thanks in all circumstances, for this is God's will for you in Christ Jesus.
1 Thessalonians 5:16–18

Jesus changed Paul's life and sent him on a mission. What mission might God have in mind for you? As you travel, be aware—as Paul was—of opportunities to tell others about Jesus. Who knows what great adventure might be waiting at the next rest stop?

HIT THE ROAD!

Saul hit the road to Damascus all right, but not the way he intended. God intercepted Saul on his way to arrest Christians. A blinding light knocked him to the ground. God had finally had Saul's attention! Read the story from Acts 9:1–19 and draw the scene in the frame below.

JAILBREAK

Everywhere Paul went, he told people about Jesus. Sometimes, people listened to the Good News and responded with joy. Other times, they got angry. In Philippi, preaching about Jesus got Paul thrown in jail, but God miraculously broke him out. Help Paul get through the maze below and get out of jail.

Paul: A Man Of Many Words

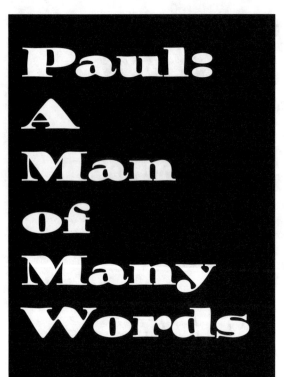

Did you know that the apostle Paul wrote more books of the Bible than anyone else?

When Paul traveled and introduced people to Jesus, he started churches. Then, when he moved on to a new place, Paul took care of his new churches by writing letters to them. We have those letters (sometimes called epistles)—along with letters from other apostles—in the New Testament, starting with the book of Romans.

Find words about the life of this man of many words in the puzzle across the page.

Word List

Saul	Ephesus	preaching
Paul	Barnabus	Gentiles
Damascus	Timothy	light
missionary	Rome	travel
tentmaker	jail	blind
Philippi	Corinth	epistles
Athens	Berea	

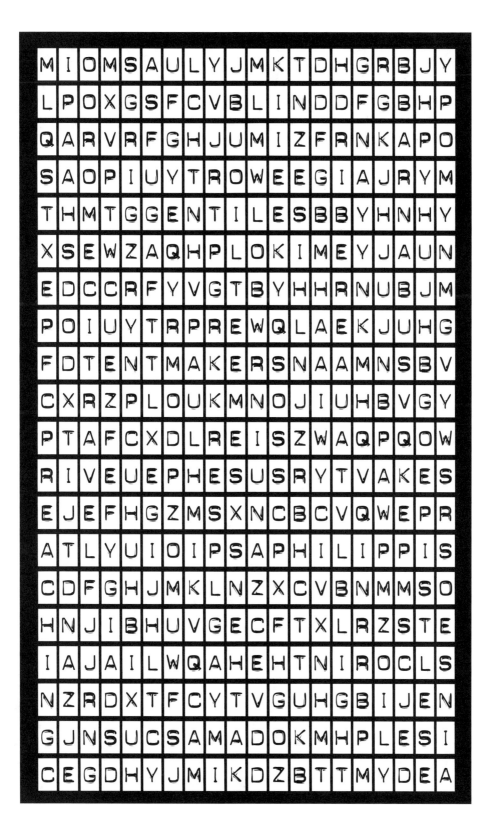

M	I	O	M	S	A	U	L	Y	J	M	K	T	D	H	G	R	B	J	Y
L	P	O	X	G	S	F	C	V	B	L	I	N	D	D	F	G	B	H	P
Q	A	R	V	R	F	G	H	J	U	M	I	Z	F	R	N	K	A	P	O
S	A	O	P	I	U	Y	T	R	O	W	E	E	G	I	A	J	R	Y	M
T	H	M	T	G	G	E	N	T	I	L	E	S	B	B	Y	H	N	H	Y
X	S	E	W	Z	A	Q	H	P	L	O	K	I	M	E	Y	J	A	U	N
E	D	C	C	R	F	Y	V	G	T	B	Y	H	H	R	N	U	B	J	M
P	O	I	U	Y	T	R	P	R	E	W	Q	L	A	E	K	J	U	H	G
F	D	T	E	N	T	M	A	K	E	R	S	N	A	A	M	N	S	B	V
C	X	R	Z	P	L	O	U	K	M	N	O	J	I	U	H	B	V	G	Y
P	T	A	F	C	X	D	L	R	E	I	S	Z	W	A	Q	P	Q	O	W
R	I	V	E	U	E	P	H	E	S	U	S	R	Y	T	V	A	K	E	S
E	J	E	F	H	G	Z	M	S	X	N	C	B	C	V	Q	W	E	P	R
A	T	L	Y	U	I	O	I	P	S	A	P	H	I	L	I	P	P	I	S
C	D	F	G	H	J	M	K	L	N	Z	X	C	V	B	N	M	M	S	O
H	N	J	I	B	H	U	V	G	E	C	F	T	X	L	R	Z	S	T	E
I	A	J	A	I	L	W	Q	A	H	E	H	T	N	I	R	O	C	L	S
N	Z	R	D	X	T	F	C	Y	T	V	G	U	H	G	B	I	J	E	N
G	J	N	S	U	C	S	A	M	A	D	O	K	M	H	P	L	E	S	I
C	E	G	D	H	Y	J	M	I	K	D	Z	B	T	T	M	Y	D	E	A

You'll find the solution on p. 76.

Be Like a

Whenever Paul visited a new town, he began by preaching in the synagogue. He wanted to persuade God's people that Jesus was the Messiah they'd long been waiting for. One of the cities where Paul went was Berea. Acts 17 tells us that the Bereans listened to Paul and then "examined the Scriptures every day to see if what Paul said was true." How cool! They took God's truth seriously.

Today we hear a lot of things that sound like truth. Some things we hear even sound like they come from the Bible. Like the Bereans, we need to be smart about what's in God's Word and what's not.

Across the page you'll find statements that sound like they're from the Bible. Some of them are straight from God's Word. Some of them have been changed just slightly—they're close to the truth, but not quite true. Some of the statements aren't in the Bible at all. Can you tell which is which? Get opinions from your whole family. Circle T for "true" next to the statements that come from the Bible and F for "false" next to the ones that don't. Then check the answers on pp. 76–77 and see what you learn.

Berean!

Statement 1

You should honor your Father and mother.   T   F

Statement 2

Saul and Paul were twins.   T   F

Statement 3

Cleanliness is next to godliness.   T   F

Statement 4

Don't lie unless it helps keep the peace.   T   F

Statement 5

God helps those who help themselves.   T   F

Statement 6

Jesus told Peter, "From now on you will catch fish."   T   F

Statement 7

Jesus felt all the same temptations we do.   T   F

Statement 8

Jesus said, "Find your own way to God."   T   F

Statement 9

Paul told Christians to put on a suit of spiritual armor.   T   F

Art in Athens

Before Paul was done preaching in Berea, he got run out of town by some people who didn't like him. The next place he went was Athens, a city full of idols. Paul chose a unique way to introduce the people of Athens to Jesus. He looked at their artwork and found a way to relate it to the Good News.

Below, create a path that answers each question about Paul's time in Athens. You can follow the letters in any direction as long as they're connected by a line to the next letter. You won't use all the letters in the puzzle. (See Acts 17 for a little help.)

Paul found a statue with a weird title. It said, **"TO ...**

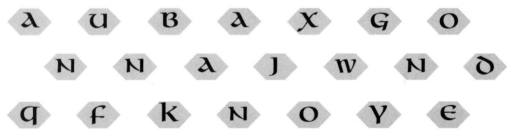

Paul quoted some of the Athenians' own poets, who said, **"WE ARE ...**

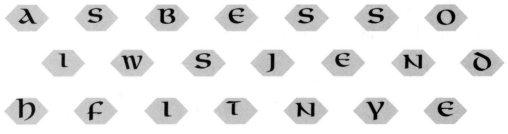

You'll find the answers on p. 77.

Tentmaking in Corinth

Another stop on Paul's big road trip was Corinth. There, he found two friends who had the same occupation as he did—they made tents for a living. He stayed and worked with them for a while and built up the church in Corinth.

Use the decoder below to discover the names of Paul's tentmaking friends.

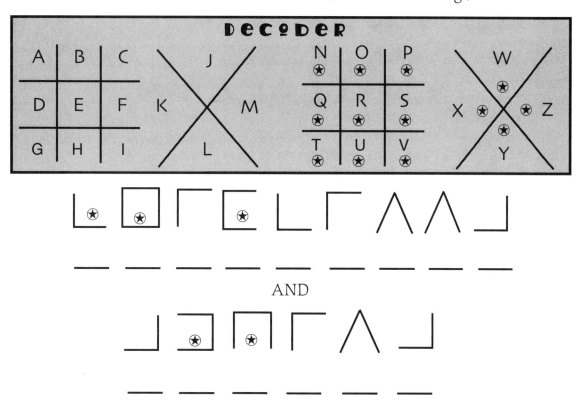

AND

You'll find the answers on p. 77.

Uproar in Ephesus

When Paul's journey brought him to Ephesus, he created quite a stir. As the people there came to know Jesus, they stopped buying things from the temple of the false goddess Artemis. The silversmiths who sold stuff there were upset because they were losing money. Because of this, a riot started, and Paul decided it was time to get out of town. Before you follow Paul out of Ephesus, see how many words you can make from the letters in

ARTEMIS OF THE EPHESIANS

Challenge a friend to see who can come up with the most words.

Praising in Prison

When you go on a road trip, it always ends at home. But Paul's road trip ended when he was thrown in prison in Rome for preaching about Jesus. Even there, he stayed strong and remained faithful to God. He was willing to make a difference, even in prison.

Unscramble these words that have to do with being in jail.

1. shcian _____

2. lcel _____

3. rabs _____

4. klhscaes _____

5. ripsnore _____

6. ugrdsa _____

7. dab oodf _____

8. on dremofe _____

9. dbonu _____

10. rsreadet _____

You'll find the answers on p. 78.

JOHN'S SUPERNATURAL JOURNEY

After Jesus rose from the dead and went back to heaven, his friends spent the rest of their lives telling everyone they knew about him. Many of them were thrown into prison or punished in other ways for telling people about Jesus. The apostle John was banished to an island called Patmos for his testimony about Jesus. Talk about a crazy trip! And from there, things got even crazier.

One day as John was worshipping on Patmos, God took him on a supernatural journey to heaven. That's right, one minute he was praying on an island and the next minute he was in the throne room of God. What he saw there was so spectacular that he barely had words to describe it—a city made of jewels with streets of gold. Rainbows, blazing lamps, and angels with eyes all over their bodies.

60

Though John was blown away by what he saw on his journey, he wrote it down as best he could. His record of his trip to heaven is what we call the book of Revelation. When we read it, we can get some idea of the wonderful road trip God has planned for all his children one day—our final trip to heaven.

John gave us an amazing window on what heaven will be like for those who believe in Jesus. There will be no tears, no sadness, no night. The glory of God will be the only light we need. We will have new, heavenly bodies. We'll be in the presence of Jesus and his people who have gone before. Sound cool? It gets better: It never ends!

I saw the Holy City, the new Jerusalem, coming down out of heaven from God, prepared as a bride beautifully dressed for her husband. And I heard a loud voice from the throne saying, "Now the dwelling of God is with men, and he will live with them. They will be his people, and God himself will be with them and be their God. He will wipe every tear from their eyes. There will be no more death or mourning or crying or pain, for the old order of things has passed away." Revelation 21:2–4

A new heaven and a new earth where everyone worships God. We can hardly wait! Think of the best time you ever had—a place that was so wonderful, where you were having a such a great time that you never wanted to leave. Now multiply that by billions and you begin to get a picture of what awaits those who love Jesus.

Stay true.

Come quickly, Lord Jesus!

Not Your Everyday Trip

Just imagine. Suppose you, like John, could be swept up out of time and space on a spectacular supernatural journey. What would it be like? With your traveling buddies or a group of friends, take turns answering these questions aloud.

1. If you could see God, what's one question you would ask?

2. Name five people you're looking forward to seeing in heaven.

3. Tickle your five senses. What will heaven smell like? Sound like? Will you taste or touch anything? What will you hear?

4. What will be the most surprising thing in heaven?

5. If you could write one letter from heaven, who would you want to write? What would you say?

6. How do you think God's light compares to daylight?

7. What do you think angels are really like?

8. What's one thing that really makes you look forward to heaven?

SPARKLERS!

In Revelation 21, John wrote about the jewels that are used to make the Holy City in heaven. Some of these jewels are listed below, but the jewelry cutter got a little carried away and cut out part of their names. Can you fill in the missing parts of the letters to discover some of the jewels that make up heaven?

JASPER

SAPPHIRE

EMERALD

TOPAZ

AMETHYST

You'll find the answers on p. 78.

fantastic creatures

Have you ever traveled to a new place with strange sights—plants and animals you've never seen before? On his journey to heaven, John saw some very odd creatures, unlike any he had ever seen on earth. In Revelation 4, he wrote about them.

In the list below, write "yes" next to the descriptions John actually wrote. Write "no" next to any made-up descriptions that don't really come from Revelation. (The first two are done for you.) Check your answers on p. 78. Then draw a picture of how you imagine one of the heavenly creatures John described.

description	answer
1. Looked like a lion	Yes, this is from Revelation
2. Looked like a zebra	No, this one is made up
3. Had seven heads	
4. Looked like an ox	
5. Had twenty toes	
6. Had six wings	
7. Had green hair	
8. Had the face of a man	
9. Looked like a flying eagle	
10. Had a purple nose	
11. Was covered with eyes, even under its wings	
12. Had spikes on its back	

fantastic creatures

your creature

Revelation Mind Bender

We don't know much about the elders John mentioned in Revelation, but let's pretend four of them are named Matthew, Mark, Luke, and Zerubbabel. And let's say they're wearing crowns of silver, gold, platinum, and diamonds. Use the clues below to figure out which elder wears which crown.

CLUES

1. Luke doesn't wear a crown of silver.

2. The elder whose crown is made of diamonds isn't named after one of the four gospels.

3. Matthew's crown and Luke's crown appear the same color, even though they're made of different metals.

4. The elder whose crown is silver and the elder whose crown is gold have names that start with the same letter.

	Matthew	Mark	Luke	Zerubbabel
Silver				
Gold				
Platinum				
Diamonds				

You'll find the answers on p. 79.

A Game of Sevens

On his trip to the heavenly realms, John saw many things in groups of seven—seven angels, seven trumpets, seven seals, seven bowls. Below are some common phrases that all contain seven of something. The first letter of each word in the phrase is given to you. Can you figure out what the phrase is?

1. Seven w_____ of the w_____.

2. S_____ W_____ and the Seven D_____.

3. Seven d_____ s_____.

4. S_____ t_____ seven you should f_____.

5. Seven d_____ in a w_____.

You'll find the answers on p. 79.

RHYME TIME!

Each word or phrase below rhymes with something John encountered on his supernatural journey. Can you name the rhyming words?

1. Teacher _____

2. Mold _____

3. Pretty _____

4. Stone _____

5. Jam _____

6. Brown _____

7. Strange bell _____

8. Spools _____

9. Welders _____

10. Lobes _____

You'll find the answers on p. 79.

ALL THE ANSWERS

ABRAHAM'S JOURNEY, P. 6

S	O	D	O	M	H	E	H	I	O	K	O	S	Q	R	T	N	N	M	H
A	S	B	V	C	X	Z	R	H	Y	J	I	O	A	Q	E	E	R	T	K
M	N	Y	A	Q	W	U	Y	M	C	F	G	H	K	G	W	A	Z	B	H
P	M	O	B	L	E	S	S	I	N	G	U	B	E	Y	V	R	C	R	X
E	Z	W	A	Q	E	C	T	A	R	V	T	V	B	Y	N	U	M	I	K
L	O	P	A	L	S	K	D	R	J	F	H	G	O	O	F	Q	A	Z	W
S	X	E	D	C	R	H	F	A	L	T	A	R	V	T	L	G	B	Y	H
N	U	J	M	I	O	K	O	S	L	P	A	A	Q	P	O	W	O	E	I
R	U	T	Y	A	A	L	S	K	D	J	D	L	H	F	C	G	M	Z	N
X	N	C	R	B	V	L	P	M	K	O	O	N	J	I	K	I	N	G	S
B	H	A	U	V	G	Y	C	A	B	R	A	M	F	T	S	X	D	R	Z
S	H	E	E	A	W	K	S	H	D	E	J	S	N	S	R	I	M	X	E
P	Q	R	S	X	B	N	M	U	S	G	B	H	P	O	I	U	Y	T	R
G	F	S	I	A	C	A	M	E	L	B	V	C	S	D	R	E	H	N	H
Q	A	E	M	B	G	T	Y	H	O	N	J	U	I	K	K	I	A	O	L
W	C	T	O	N	U	K	O	F	T	B	U	J	N	I	K	M	R	S	D
F	R	B	R	A	C	T	N	J	I	M	K	Z	S	F	Y	N	A	I	P
E	G	Y	P	T	R	H	N	A	A	N	A	C	B	H	U	E	N	T	B
A	S	C	R	E	D	Z	S	C	V	X	R	B	Y	H	J	F	I	U	A
G	A	F	S	D	L	G	K	H	J	M	V	N	C	B	X	L	A	N	D

TOO MANY TO COUNT, P. 7

In a little under 475 years, John will have more than one million descendants. And that's if each person in his family has only two kids. Since we know that Abraham's grandson Jacob had more than twelve kids, we can bet that his family reached a million much more quickly!

EGYPTIAN MIND BENDER, PP. 8-9

Shua kept the cattle; Beruch kept the camels; Gad kept the goats; Hosea kept the sheep.

SWITCHEROOS, P. 11

1. Saul/Paul
2. Eliakim/Jehoiakim
3. Jacob/Israel
4. Mattaniah/Zedekiah
5. Simon/Peter
6. All believers in Christ

NORTH AND SOUTH, EAST AND WEST, pp. 12-13

The points on the walk form a cross.

WE'RE SO OUTTA HERE CROSSWORD, pp. 16-17

down	across
1. Pharaoh	2. Magicians
2. Moses	5. Plagues
3. Aaron	6. Frogs
4. Sacrifice	8. Red Sea
6. Firstborn	11. Staff
7. Hail	12. Blood
9. Slaves	14. Angel
10. God	15. Free
13. Darkness	16. Nile
17. Lamb	

CARRY ON, P. 18

Simeon's family: Children carried items that began with the same letter as their names.

Joshua's family: Children whose names began with consonants carried items that began with consonants. Children whose names started with vowels carried items that began with vowels.

WHINE-ATHON, P. 19

1. Are we there yet?
2. Can we stop for lunch?
3. I have to go to the bathroom!
4. I'm bored!
5. He's touching me!

EXODUS BY THE NUMBERS, pp. 20-21

A. 83
B. 3
C. 137
D. 10
E. 600,000
F. 430
G. 600
H. 10

STONES OF REMEMBRANCE, P. 22

"The hand of the Lord is powerful" (Joshua 4:24).

THE BIG TEN, PP. 24-25

Cracking the first code: The first number in each pair represents a commandment. The second number represents a letter within that commandment. So 2-3 means the third letter in the second commandment.

The solution is "Love the Lord with all your heart and with all your soul and with all your mind."

Cracking the second code: "Do not murder" is the sixth commandment. To create a decoder for this puzzle, each letter is moved six spaces to the right, like this:

Code	U V W X Y Z A B C D E F G H I J K L M N O P Q R S T
Actual Letter	A B C D E F G H I J K L M N O P Q R S T U V W X Y Z

The solution is "Love your neighbor as yourself."

SETTLE DOWN! P. 29

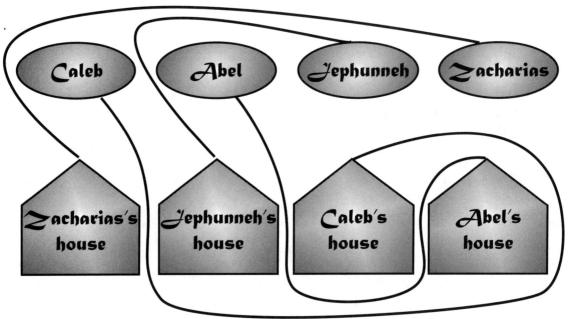

ALL THE KING'S MEN, P. 30

only vegetables

RAAAAAARRR! P. 31

1. mane
2. sharp claws
3. pointy teeth
4. cat family
5. king of beasts
6. Africa
7. cubs

OL' KING NEB, P. 32

He lived like an animal.

THERE AND BACK AGAIN, P. 33

boomerang
letter or mail
retriever
baseball player
goose

THE SURPRISING SAVIOR, P. 38

1. sun
2. easy
3. rare
4. violent
5. all
6. never
7. terrible
Last question: servant

ON THE ROAD AGAIN, P. 37

another dream

GOT FOOD? PP. 42-43

A (5000)	=5000
÷ B (5)	=1000
÷ C (2)	=500
x 9	=4500
+ D (12)	=4512
- E (4000)	=512
+ 13	=525
÷ F (7)	=75
- D (12)	=68
- G (7)	=56
- D (12)	=49
+ 1	=50
x 400	=18,000

THE HARDEST ROAD, P. 46

1. Judas Iscariot
2. Peter
3. Pontius Pilate
4. Mary Magdalene
5. Barabbas
6. Simon from Cyrene

JOURNEYING WITH JESUS, P. 47

1 CROSS
1 CHRISTMAS
2 SEAOFGALILEE
3 REPENT
3 RISE
4 EGYPT
5 TEACH
6 DIED
7 MAN
8 SACRIFICED
9 NAILS
10 SERVE
10 SAVIOR
11 RABBI
12 MIRACLE
13 GOD

PAUL, A MAN OF MANY WORDS, PP. 52-53

M	I	O	M	S	A	U	L	Y	J	M	K	T	D	H	G	R	B	J	Y
L	P	O	X	G	S	F	C	V	B	L	I	N	D	D	F	G	B	H	P
Q	A	R	V	R	F	G	H	J	U	M	I	Z	F	R	N	K	A	P	O
S	A	O	P	I	U	Y	T	R	O	W	E	E	G	I	A	J	R	Y	M
T	H	M	T	G	G	E	N	T	I	L	E	S	B	B	Y	H	N	H	Y
X	S	E	W	Z	A	Q	H	P	L	O	K	I	M	E	Y	J	A	U	N
E	D	C	C	R	F	Y	V	G	T	B	Y	H	H	R	N	U	B	J	M
P	O	I	U	Y	T	R	P	R	E	W	Q	L	A	E	K	J	U	H	G
F	D	T	E	N	T	M	A	K	E	R	S	N	A	A	M	N	S	B	V
C	X	R	Z	P	L	O	U	K	M	N	O	J	I	U	H	B	V	G	Y
P	T	A	F	C	X	D	L	R	E	I	S	Z	W	A	Z	P	Q	O	W
R	I	V	E	U	E	P	H	E	S	U	S	R	Y	T	V	A	K	E	S
E	J	E	F	H	G	Z	M	S	X	N	C	B	C	C	V	Q	W	P	R
A	T	L	Y	U	I	O	I	P	S	A	P	H	I	L	I	P	P	I	S
C	D	F	G	H	J	M	K	L	N	Z	X	C	V	B	N	M	M	S	O
H	N	J	I	B	H	U	V	G	E	C	F	T	X	L	R	Z	S	T	E
I	A	J	A	I	L	W	Q	A	T	E	H	T	N	I	R	O	C	L	S
N	Z	R	D	X	T	F	C	Y	H	V	G	U	H	G	B	I	J	E	N
G	J	N	S	U	C	S	A	M	A	D	O	K	M	H	P	L	E	S	I
C	E	G	D	H	Y	J	M	I	K	D	Z	B	T	T	M	Y	D	E	A

BE LIKE A BEREAN, PP. 54-55

1. True. Exodus 20:12
2. False. Paul was Saul's new name after he believed in Jesus (Acts 13:9).
3. Not in the Bible, but being clean is a really good idea!
4. False. Exodus 20:16

5. Not in the Bible

6. False. Jesus told Peter to leave his nets and said, "From now on you will catch men" (Luke 5:11).

7. True. Hebrews 4:15

8. False. Jesus said, "I am the way and the truth and the life. No one comes to the Father except through me" (John 14:6).

9. True. Ephesians 6:10–17

ART IN ATHENS, P. 56

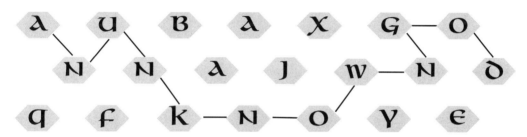

"an unknown god"

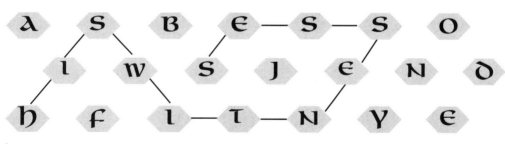

"his witnesses"

TENTMAKING IN CORINTH, P. 57

Priscilla and Aquila

PRAISING IN PRISON, P. 59

1. chains

2. cell

3. bars

4. shackles

5. prisoner

6. guards

7. bad food

8. no freedom

9. bound

10. arrested

SPARKLERS! P. 63

jasper

sapphire

emerald

topaz

amethyst

FANTASTIC CREATURES, PP. 64-65

1. Yes
2. No
3. No
4. Yes
5. No
6. Yes

7. No
8. Yes
9. Yes
10. No
11. Yes
12. No

REVELATION MIND BENDER, P. 66

	Matthew	Mark	Luke	Zerubbabel
Silver	Yes	No	No	No
Gold	No	Yes	No	No
Platinum	No	No	Yes	No
Diamonds	No	No	No	Yes

A GAME OF SEVENS, P. 67

1. Seven wonders of the world
2. Snow White and the Seven Dwarfs
3. Seven deadly sins
4. Seventy times seven you should forgive
5. Seven days in a week

RHYME TIME, P. 68

1. creature
2. gold
3. city
4. throne
5. lamb
6. crown
7. angel
8. jewels
9. elders
10. robes

The Word at Work Around the World

A vital part of Cook Communications Ministries is our international outreach, Cook Communications Ministries International (CCMI). Your purchase of this book, and of other books and Christian-growth products from Cook, enables CCMI to provide Bibles and Christian literature to people in more than 150 languages in 65 countries.

Cook Communications Ministries is a not-for-profit, self-supporting organization. Revenues from sales of our books, Bible curricula, and other church and home products not only fund our U.S. ministry, but also fund our CCMI ministry around the world. One hundred percent of donations to CCMI go to our international literature programs.

CCMI reaches out internationally in three ways:

• Our premier International Christian Publishing Institute (ICPI) trains leaders from nationally led publishing houses around the world.

• We provide literature for pastors, evangelists, and Christian workers in their national language.

• We reach people at risk—refugees, AIDS victims, street children, and famine victims—with God's Word.

Word Power, God's Power

Faith Kidz, RiverOak, Honor, Life Journey, Victor, NexGen — every time you purchase a book produced by Cook Communications Ministries, you not only meet a vital personal need in your life or in the life of someone you love, but you're also a part of ministering to José in Colombia, Humberto in Chile, Gousa in India, or Lidiane in Brazil. You help make it possible for a pastor in China, a child in Peru, or a mother in West Africa to enjoy a life-changing book. And because you helped, children and adults around the world are learning God's Word and walking in his ways.

Thank you for your partnership in helping to disciple the world. May God bless you with the power of his Word in your life.

For more information about our international ministries, visit www.ccmi.org.